Bibliographic information published by the German National Library:

The German National Library lists this publication in the National Bibliography;
detailed bibliographic data are available on the Internet at http://dnb.dnb.de .

Imprint:

Copyright © 2015 GRIN Verlag, Open Publishing GmbH
Print and binding: Books on Demand GmbH, Norderstedt Germany
ISBN: 9783668370906

This book at GRIN:

http://www.grin.com/en/e-book/350571/to-what-extent-is-debt-relief-an-essential-
precondition-to-effective-poverty

Anna Scheithauer

To what Extent is Debt Relief an Essential Precondition to Effective Poverty Reduction?

GRIN Publishing

GRIN - Your knowledge has value

Since its foundation in 1998, GRIN has specialized in publishing academic texts by students, college teachers and other academics as e-book and printed book. The website www.grin.com is an ideal platform for presenting term papers, final papers, scientific essays, dissertations and specialist books.

To what Extent is Debt Relief an Essential Precondition to Effective Poverty Reduction?

In this essay I will argue that the relationship between debt relief and poverty reduction is contingent on the relationship between conditionality and creditor-debtor responsibility. Doing so, I will focus on third generation conditionality of the Post Washington Consensus, which ties debt relief to the integration of poverty reducing policies. It is based on the idea that conditional debt cancellation will lead to policy improvements, which will boost investment and social expenditures, and consequently lead to economic growth and poverty reduction. (Dijkstra, 2008)

Doing so, I will concentrate on the political economy determinant of debt relief, asymmetric information, as it overshadows debt-overhung, crowding-out, and institution theory by far. (Johansson, 2010) I shall clarify in the first section of the paper why this is so and make reference to the broader debate. Asymmetric information - a situation, where one party in a transaction process has more or better information than the other (Bebzcuk, 2003, xi) - is also relevant with view to my claim being based on the premise that conditionality leads to adverse selection and moral hazard (Dijkstra, 2008), two classic examples of information asymmetry. The former correlates the demand for a loan (or debt relief) with the risk of potential default (on conditions) and renders the creditor, due to imperfect information, unable to reflect this calculation in the selection of candidates. The latter spreads all impacts born out of this correlation, resulting from information asymmetry and a lack of control over the debtor, across a pool of parties, so that one party's actions will affect that of all others. (Bebzcuk, 2003, 7)

In this sense, I will use the Enhanced Highly Indebted Poor Country Initiative (HIPCI II), which was launched by the IMF and World Bank (WB) embodying a major instrument of development policy linked to the realization of the Millennium Development Goals (MDGs) to illustrate how conditionality in debt relief triggers problems of adverse selection and moral hazard and, in turn, undermines poverty reduction (Dijkstra, 2008). However, I won't address the conditions' content as this would exceed the space provided for this assignment. It still needs to be born in mind though, that tensions between financing the MDGs and debt sustainability necessarily arise with program compliance. (Gunter, 2011, 52)

First, adverse selection is evidenced by the following observations: Being considered for HIPCI II assistance is tied to the fulfillment of eligibility criteria. Countries qualifying for HIPCI II assistance are then required to adopt reforms. (Berensmann, 2004, 321-322) The problems are two-fold: a) countries not meeting the criteria, regardless of their levels of poverty, won't be entitled for debt relief, and b) creditors feature defensive lending behavior by continuing to give loans to prevent default on past loans (= path-dependence) as well as to avoid admitting past mistakes regardless the degree of poverty reducing reform (Johannson, 2010, 1206).

Second, conditional debt relief spurs, on the one hand, *debtor moral hazard*. Not only will the cost of borrowing increase by enabling debtors to contract out from obligations affecting all debtors as a group (Tan, 2014, 255), but it also creates incentives for debtors to borrow in anticipation of debt relief (Easterly, 2002, 1679), which upon default and lack of punishment for non-compliance enlarges the burden of the group (Mwaba, 2005, 542-543) including the poor; through i.e. increased taxes for higher debt servicing (Easterly, 2002, 1681). On the other hand, debt relief also leads to *creditor moral hazard* since bilateral donors tend to underestimate the risks and over-lend after debt relief, usually in non-concessional ways. This not only aggravates debtor moral hazard (Arnone and Prespitero, 2013, 228), but also adds to the adverse selection problem, since creditors – now that capacity for new loans is freed - select those countries for further lending that don't have access to loans from others; which are presumably those with worse policies increasing the risk for renewed default. (Dijkstra, 2008, 120)

I will conclude that due to the absence of a legal framework to govern activities of debt relief and commercial lending (Pettifor, 2007, 138) as well as the lack of acknowledgment to make them a matter of shared responsibility by creditors and debtors alike, policy conditionality will inevitably lead to adverse selection and moral hazard rendering debt relief not more than "a necessary but insufficient condition" (Berensmann, 2004, 321) for poverty reduction.

From Conditionality towards Shared Responsibility

However multifold the literature on debt relief, only few (e.g. Easterly, 2001) would dispute that external debt is a major cause of poverty. (Berensman, 2004, 321) Efforts on debt relief have been endless but mostly with crushing results. It has been a complex issue under study on which four main theories developed inspiring the actions of creditors and donors alike.

Econometric studies have focused on how debt affects growth which in turn affects poverty. For example, Krugman and Sachs stated, when debt overhang occurs – a situation where a country's external debt exceeds its repayment ability – most of the country's output will be redirected from investment to debt servicing. Thus, through debt relief a country will regain its ability to pay, which encourages public and private investment. (Johansson, 2010, 1204) However, a reduced debt stock doesn't guarantee a government's ability to achieve growth. Arslanlap and Blaire Henry i.e. established in their comparative study of the Brady Plan and the HIPCI I, that debt overhung theory in the absence of functional economic institutions (i.e. imagine a tax base that achieves little revenue simply because the poor are too poor) falls short in providing the cure out of poverty. (2006)

Crowding-out theory, on the other hand, suggests that debt service payments not only impede growth, but crowd out spending in areas like health and education. But debt relief would in this respect only create additional fiscal space if a country had been servicing its debts before. (Johannson, 2010, 1205) Thus, debt relief and development aid need to complement each other in order for resources to be made available for social spending. However, additionality depends on the type of reallocations creditors/donors will make to their traditional aid upon debt relief, and since aid budgets are fixed aid-flows might stop or be redirected to other recipients. (Gunter, 2011, 54-58) But even if capacities were freed and additional aid provided, it remains questionable whether a government would channel its expenditures towards investments with high social returns. Clements (2005) et al found i.e. that debt relief has in most cases led to higher consumption instead of investment. And if investment would go up, it still leads to questions of adequate distribution (i.e. sectoral and population segmental) (Lumina, 2008, 5), the quality of reforms achieved, and actual correlation of such increase with debt relief and aid. (Moss, 289, 2006)

Thirdly, institutional quality and good governance are said to impact debt relief. (e.g. Asiedu, 2003) But, while Burnside and Dollar (2000) find that aid has a strong positive effect on growth in countries with sound management, and Agenor (2008) illustrates how increases in aid combined with reforms to improve the management of public resources can maximize the impact on growth and poverty reduction, Colderon et al. (2009, 79) find no effect of aid on poverty in countries with good institutions. They link their finding to the misallocation of resources to foreign firms and consultants and projects without productive value, and to policy makers prioritizing national security and domestic politics over poverty reduction.

These theories have influenced the approach the international financial institutions (IFIs) have taken in tackling the increasing debt burden of heavily indebted poor countries. However, their debt relief initiative HIPC I based on ex-post conditions containing a package of policy reforms (Structural Adjustment Programs) to be fulfilled in exchange for debt relief actually perpetuated the debt crisis. (Canel, 2009, 7-8) With view to poverty reduction, Dijkstra (2008, 69) found in a six-country study that even though social sector investment went up, aid and debt relief remained low compared to high debt payments, so that social expenditures didn't grow at the same rate or even declined.

This is not only due to the complexities discussed above, but is mainly the result of asymmetric information, or more specifically of a) adverse selection and b) moral hazard. In this respect, theory four states that a) debt relief will hardly be effective, if creditors allocate debt relief to countries with an unsustainable debt burden, rather than to countries better able and willing to increase investment, and b) debt relief encourages new loans in expectation of further debt relief, so that countries start borrowing excessively risking debt overhang anew. Hence, the investment effect sought by debt overhang, crowding-out and institution theory will be low because of information asymmetry (Johannson, 2010)

In response to a worsening debt crisis, the IMF and WB launched the HIPCI II as a follow-up on HIPCI I, which has offered greater debt relief than ever and tied the goal of sustainable development in form of quantified targets (MDGs) as a stringent condition to their assistance. This requires countries to account for how freed capacities from debt relief are channeled towards poverty reduction. (Tan, 2014, 259) To increase the effectiveness of the initiative the selectivity process was refined, whereby in a first step (decision point) countries must fulfill four conditions to be considered for assistance: 1. be eligible to borrow from the IFIs, 2. feature an unsustainable debt burden, 3. have a track-record of reform through the IMF's and WB's supported programs, 4. have developed a Poverty Reduction Strategy Paper (PRSP), and in a second step (completion point) to implement further reforms together with the PRSP for at least a year. (IMF, 2014)

However, the HIPCI II has so far only further exacerbated the debt crisis just as it has aggravated adverse selection and moral hazard, undermining the aim of poverty reduction. This is due to conditionality in general, and the HIPCI II's augmented "double conditionality" of ex-ante (decision point) and ex-post (completion point) conditions, in particular. (Dijkstra, 2008, 111).

The former are problematic in that they trigger adverse selection in various ways. The requirement of an "unsustainable debt burden" encourages only heavily indebted poor countries (HIPCs) to apply for debt relief. This might be promulgated by proponents of debt overhang theory, but it comes at high cost. Not only tend HIPCs to exhibit worse policies than non-HIPCs and, thus, to be less willing to invest their freed resources, but also tend to feature lower levels of poverty than some of the non-HIPCS (i.e. India). (Dijkstra, 2008, 114) Adverse selection is further aggravated by the requirement of a track-record of reform with the IMF and WB. This points to path-dependence, whereby debt relief is mainly provided to those countries, whose debt was forgiven under HIPC I. (Freytag, Pehnelt, 2009, 66)

This raises two concerns: First, ex-ante selectivity brings about issues of inequity. Not only miss non-HIPCs, despite high poverty levels, out on the chance for debt cancellation (Gunter, 2002, 7), but also some of the HIPCs struggle to qualify for debt relief under these stringent conditions. (Bernsmann, 2004, 322) Consequently it is mostly the same group of low income countries, that are eligible for assistance. (Chauvin and Kraay in Dijkstra, 2008, 114) This is evidenced i.e. by the WB's Country Policy and Institutional Index scores upon which aid allocations are based (Dijkstra, 2008, 115). Such path-dependence by creditors might furthermore come at the detriment to non-qualifying countries in form of aid re-allocations as donors' fixed budgets force them to re-direct their funds to participating HIPCs. (Gunter, 2011, 54-58) This leaves the poor in other low-income countries not only with a missed opportunity for debt relief, but also with a loss in additional aid flows, impeding their chances for development respectively poverty reduction.

Second, ex-post conditionality tied to the implementation of the MDGs requires beyond the investment of freed capacities additional aid (Greenhill, 2002, 8), usually granted in form of new loans. However, if a country's poverty reduction strategies are not or only insufficiently carried out, or/and fail to encourage investment and growth, renewed default will be certain.

Such possibility notwithstanding, the IFIs have proven to engage in defensive lending by consciously supporting bad record countries with new loans. According to Buwlow and Rogoff (2005), and Prespitero (2009) et al. such defensive lending is due to the IFIs' desire to prevent default on past loans as well as to avoid admitting past policy errors (i.e. lending to corrupt governments). This response on potential defaults with new loans contradicts debt-overhang theory (Freytag, 2009, 64) and inevitably comes at the cost of poverty reduction. This shows that adverse selection is not only a matter of debtor conduct, but also of donor responsibility. (Hertz, 2005)

In this sense, Hanlon (2006) suggests in his country study on Iraq that loans made to repressive regimes should be viewed as "illegitimate" debt, and be forgiven upon acquisition of acceptable policies. This would discipline creditors and prevent further lending to oppressive governments. Hanlon's approach falls short, though, in providing a feasible solution to issues of adverse selection due to the draw-backs of institution theory outlined before, whereby finding agreement on what constitutes an "illegitimate" regime or "good" policies (Easterly, 2001) would figure but one of the challenges.

Nevertheless, a shifting focus from debtor conduct to creditor responsibility shows that adverse selection is also a supply side problem. In this respect, Dijkstra (2008, 46) points to a conflict of interest that has helped maintain the cycle of new loans: Despite debtor non-compliance with programs renewed assistance is certain due to IMF interests in obtaining funds from the WB and bilateral programs. These are issued upon conclusion of new IMF agreements and comprise free resources for the payment of past loans. This highlights creditors' needs conflicting with the aims of HIPCI II resulting from the IFIs' dual function of "gatekeeper" and creditor. (Dijkstra, 2008, 115)

Conditionality and adverse selection are thereby closely linked to moral hazard, a further example of asymmetric information, spurred by debtor misconduct and lack of creditor responsibility. *Debtor moral hazard* is triggered by ex-ante conditionality in that it establishes a pool of high-risk HIPCI II participants. As they face an unsustainable debt burden chances for improvements in investment and consequential growth are slim. The risk of default further increases due to ex-post conditionality requiring the implementation of PRSPs directing sources to sectors delivering social rather than economic returns, and possibly the taking-on of new loans. This increases the cost of borrowing, which affects all debtors as a group, including non-participating countries. (Tan, 2014, 255)

Such burden-sharing also creates incentives for debtors to borrow in anticipation of debt relief expecting renewed cancellation of loans. (Easterly, 2002, 1679). This further enlarges the burden of the group as sanctions on non-compliance are rarely imposed (Mwaba, 2005, 542-543) which, in turn, puts constraints on poverty reduction as the increase in debt service will need to be recovered, i.e. through an increase in taxes (Easterly, 2002, 1681), a decrease in social expenditures (Gunter, 2002, 8), and similar measures that could potentially hurt the poor. This is particularly troublesome with view to the poor of those developing countries (i.e. Brazil, South Africa) including HIPCs that figure amongst creditors not being exempt from burden-sharing. (Gunter, 2002, 12)

Apart from debtor moral hazard, HIPCI II conditionality also leads to *creditor moral hazard* as debt relief creates borrowing space and attracts new lending opportunities especially from bilateral donors offering non-concessional loans. In this sense, debt relief subsidizes such donors, and creates a free-riding problem among creditors, which undermines all efforts of the IFIs for debt sustainability. (Arnone and Prespitero, 2013, 228) Here, additional complexities arise through the emergence of new donors (i.e. China), which through their often non-concessional aid are accused of encouraging bad policies and lowering standards, adding to an increasing debt burden. (Woods, 2008) The IFIs have, to the detriment of the poor, responded with punishing debtors that engage in these new loans with harsher conditions and a reduction in aid flows. (Dijkstra, 2008, 120

However, it needs to be pointed out that also the IFIs contribute to the collective-action problem when free-riding on debt relief of bilateral donors. This adds to adverse selectivity in that HIPCs without access to loans from bilateral creditors are most likely those with worse policies, and consequentially the ones most likely to default anew. (Dijkstra, 2008, 120) Not only is such behavior facilitated by the absence of a legal framework for international lending, but also reveals the political nature of debt relief (Tan, 2014)

Conclusion

The preceding paragraphs have shown the mutually reinforcing nature of conditionality, adverse selection and moral hazard, which renders conditional debt relief necessary but insufficient to improve standards for the poor. (Woods, 2008) The HIPCI II criteria in particular embody quite the opposite of an improved selectivity process for targeting the poor. They deny the poor in non-eligible countries the chance for poverty reduction, lead to higher grants for countries with worse policies, and impose more conditions (sanctions) on countries with better policies benefiting from non-conditional bilateral aid flows, adding to moral hazard and adverse selection.

In this respect, some authors question whether debt relief should be linked to the MDGs at all. (i.e. Dijkstra, 2008) But considering this paper has shown that the relationship between debt relief and poverty reduction is highly contingent on the relationship between conditionality and creditor-debtor responsibility, one should rather question the means over the desired outcome. In this sense, it might be concluded that by regarding debt relief as a matter of shared responsibility, a stronger emphasis on the rule of law deepening MDG8 on the development of a global partnership (UN, 2014) could essentially help reduce issues of adverse selection and moral hazard, and, in turn, increase the effectiveness of poverty reduction through debt relief.

Bibliography

Agénor , Pierre-Richard; Bayraktar Nihal, El Aynaoui Karim. (2008) Roads out of Poverty? Assessing the Links Between Aid, Public investment, Growth, and Poverty reduction, Journal of Development Economics, Vol. 86, pp. 277–295

Arnone, Marc, and Prespitero, Andrea. (2013) "Some Proposals for a Comprehensive Approach to Debt Sustainability And Debt Relief", *Debt Relief Initiatives: Policy Design and Outcomes*, Ashgate Publishing, Ltd.

Arslanalp, Serkan and Balire Henry, Peter (2006) "Debt Relief", Working Paper 12187, NBER Working Paper Series, National Bureau of Economic Research, MA/USA

Asiedu, Elizabeth. (2003) "Debt Relief and Institutional Reform: A Focus on Heavily Indebted Poor Countries", The Quarterly Review of Economics and Finance Vol. 43, pp. 614–626

Bebczuk, Ricardo N. (2003) "An Introduction to Asymmetric Information Problems in Financial Markets", *Asymmetric Information in Financial Markets: Introduction and Applications*, Cambridge University Press, pp. 3-16

Burnside, Craig and, Dollar, David. (2000) "Aid, Growth, the Incentive Regime and Poverty Reduction", Gilbert, Christopher, L. and Vines, David, *The World Bank: Structure and Policies*, Cambridge University Press, pp. 210-223

Berensmann, Kathrin. (2004) New Ways of Achieving Debt Sustainability beyond the Enhanced HIPC Initiative, Intereconomics, November/December, Vol. 39, Issue 6, pp 321-330

Dijkstra, A. Geske. (2008) *The Impact of International Debt Relief,* Routledge: USA/Canada

Bulow, Jeremy, and Rogoff, Kenneth (2005). "Grants Versus Loans for Development Banks", American Economic Review, Vol. 95, No. 2, pp. 393–397.

Calderon, Cecilia; Chong, Alberto; Gradstein, Mark. (2009) "Can Foreign Aid Reduce Income Inequality and Poverty?", Public Choice, Vol. 140, pp. 59–84

Canel, Jonathan. (2009) "Debt Relief But at What Cost? Balancing Sustainability With Poverty Reduction in Debt Relief Conditions", Stanford Journal of International Relations, Fall Vol. XI/No. 1, pp. 6-15

Clements, Benedict, Bhattacharya, Rina, & Nguyen, Toan Quoc. (2005) "Can debt relief boost   growth in poor countries?" IMF Economic Issues No. 34. Washington, DC: International   Monetary Fund.

Easterly, William (2001). "Think Again: Debt Relief", Foreign Policy, Vol. 127, pp. 20-28

Easterly, Wiliam (2002) "How Did Heavily Indebted Poor Countries Become Heavily Indebted? Reviewing Two Decades of Debt Relief", World Development, Vol. 30, No. 10, pp. 1677– 1696

Freytag, Andreas, and Pehnelt, Gernot. (2009) "Debt Relief and Governance Quality in Developing Countries," World Development, Vol. 37, No. 1, pp. 62–80

Greenhill, Romilly. (2002) "The Unbreakable Link – Debt Relief and the Millennium Development Goals", A Report from Jubilee Research, New Economics Foundation, London: UK

Gunter, Bernhard. (2002) "What's Wrong with the HIPC Initiative and What's Next?", Development Policy Review, Vol. 20, No. 1, pp. 5-24

Gunter, Bernhard G. (2011) "Achieving the MDGs and Ensuring Debt Sustainability," Third World Quarterly, Vol. 32, No. 1, pp. 45-63

Hanlon, Joseph. (2006) "'Illegitimate' Loans: Lenders, Not Borrowers, Are Responsible", Third World Quarterly, Vol. 27, No. 2. pp. 211-226

Hertz, Noreena (2005) "Why We Must Defuse The Debt Threat", Contributions to Political Economy, Vol. 24, pp. 123–133

International Monetary Fund. (2014) "Factsheet: Debt Relief Under the Heavily Indebted Poor Countries (HIPC) Initiative", viewed: 5 December 2014 https://www.imf.org/external/np/exr/facts/hipc.htm

Johannson, Pernilla. (2010) "Debt Relief, Investment and Growth", World Development Vol. 38, No. 9, pp. 1204–1216

Lumina, Cephas. (2008) "Foreign Debt and Poverty: Exploring the Linkages In the Context of Human Rights", Paper presented to the 2008 Social Forum of the Human Rights Council, Geneva/Switzerland, 1-3 September

Moss, Todd. (2006) "Briefing: The G8's Multilateral Debt Relief Initiative And Poverty Reduction in Sub-Saharan Africa", African Affairs, Vol. 105, No. 419, pp. 285–293

Mwaba, Andrew (2005) "Beyond HIPC: What are the Prospects for Debt Sustainability?", African Development Bank, Blackwell Publishing Ltd, Oxford/UK and MA/USA

Pettifor, Ann. (2007) "Debt Cancellation, Lender Responsibility & Poor Country Empowerment", Review of African Political Economy, Vol. 27, No. 83, pp. 138-144

Presbitero, Andrea. (2009) "Debt-relief Effectiveness and Institution-Building", Development Policy Review, Vol. 27, No.5, pp. 529–559

Tan, Celine (2014) "Reframing the Debate: Debt Relief Initiative and New Normative Values in the Governance of Third World Debt", International Journal of Law in Context, Vol. 10, pp. 249-272

United Nations (2014), "We can end Poverty – Millennium Development Goals and Beyond 2015", viewed: 5. December 2014, http://www.un.org/millenniumgoals/global.shtml

Woods, Ngaire. (2008) "Whose aid? Whose influence?: China, Emerging Donors and the Silent Revolution in Development Assistance", International Affairs, Vol. 84, No. 6, pp. 1205-1221

YOUR KNOWLEDGE HAS VALUE

- We will publish your bachelor's and master's thesis, essays and papers

- Your own eBook and book - sold worldwide in all relevant shops

- Earn money with each sale

Upload your text at www.GRIN.com and publish for free